SEA

AFTER

60

101 SEXUAL POSITIONS-

YOU CAN ABSOLUTELY

POSITIVELY

FORGET ABOUT!

Cover and page design by Cool Journals Studios - Copyright 2019

TABLE OF CONTENTS

USE THE REMAINDER OF BOOK AS A PERSONAL JOURNAL TO REMINISCE ABOUT THE HOT SEX YOU USE TO HAVE. ENJOY!

Made in the USA
Las Vegas, NV
15 November 2024

11821837R10059